by: Rashelle Rey

I AM WHAT GOD
SAYS I AM

MP

MOCY PUBLISHING
WWW.MOCYPUBLISHING.COM

Detroit, Michigan

Printed by CreateSpace, An Amazon.com Company

I AM What God Says I Am

ISBN 978-1-940831-22-0

Published by Mocy Publishing, LLC.
Website: www.mocypublishing.com
Email: info@mocypublishing.com

I was born in Birmingham, AL.....I grew up in Detroit, MI

This book will minister to the broken hearted, the wounded spirit those that are Bound in their spirit, those that want move forward in life but can't because of life situations.
My earnest prayer is that the spirit of god will minister to your spirit I pray that you find healing in your mind in your soul. Most of all, receive the love of god in your heart, and to truly know that the father cares for you (us).

Isaiah 61 *for the spirit of the lord is upon me*. The lord has chosen me to tell good news to the poor and to comfort those who are sad. He sent me to tell the captives and prisoners that they have been set free. He sent me to announce that the time has come for the lord to show his kindness, when our god will punish evil people. He hasn't me to comfort those that are sad, those in Zion who mourn. God says I will take away the ashes on their head, and I will give them a crown. I will take away their sadness, and I will give them the oil of happiness. I will take away their sorrow, and I will give them celebration clothes. He sent me to name them Good Trees and The Lords Wonderful Plant.

May you be enriched and forever Blesses in Jesus name
I AM WHAT GOD SAYS I AM

I'll like to share that I was once bound, hurt, disappointed, rejected, and sexually abused. I'll like to put emphasis on a few things that the Spirit has been dealing with me about, and I decided to write a book. The late Bishop Stacks appeared before me years ago saying that the Lord was going to use me to write one day. I have always been a person to write my thoughts. When I was younger, I won first place more than once with my writing skills.

Pre-conventional means moral development. Studies show that most nine-year-old children don't have a personal moral code. Instead, they are shaped by the standards of adults. Our conduct or morals and views on life come from how we were raised, and being born in sin, and shaped in iniquity. The standards that our parents have instilled in us were taught to us in our childhood.

There are a lot of people hurting in today's society as well as the church world. We are hurting because of certain things that we may have seen or experienced and most of us haven't dealt with those issues. We hide behind so many things whether it be drugs, sex, self-destructive behavior, makeup, money, clothes, alcohol, food, or gambling. I mean the list goes on; whatever we can find comfort in that will suppress the issues.

Because of these issues that we carry in our hearts, it allows sin to continuously knock us down. You probably are wondering how and why. Well, the answer to your question is because sin hurts and it blocks what God says we are in him. Once we come to the full knowledge and revelation of who we are in Christ, nothing by any means can stop us.

A lot of times we try to hide the pain and deal with it in our own way, and it's impossible because it comes right back and haunts us. Sometimes we don't know to go to God. Most of us didn't grow up in a Christian household, and church was somewhere in the household, but not in the proper capacity. But today the father says, "come to me all those that are heavy laden and I will give you rest. Come with all your issues; come with your imperfectness."

Jeremiah 1-5 says,"before I formed you in your mother's womb I knew you. Before you were born, I appointed you."

Psalms 139 14-17 says, "I will praise thee for I am fearfully and wonderfully made. Marvelous are thy works and that my soul knows very well. My frame was not hidden from you when I was made in secret and skillfully wrought in the lowest parts of the earth. Your eyes saw my substance, being yet unformed. And in your book they all were written for me, the days fashioned for me. When as yet there were none of them." How precious also is your thoughts unto me O God! How great is the sum of them?

So with that being said God knew and knows everything about us. He knows the things that we are going to experience, and he knows that we can't carry these issues. That's why he says we must stay connected to the Father once we come into the knowledge of salvation. God says, " without him we can't do anything." We can't produce the fruit that he has called us to bear. We stay connected through prayer. It's okay that sometimes we don't know what to say ....Because the flip side to that is that he will make intercession for us, for the Spirit knows all things...Let's not just allow God to deal with the surface of things; God is bigger than that. He loves us so much that he wants to get down to the root and the source of things and clean us up...If you stay in prayer long enough and seek him with your whole heart, there's no way you can ever be the same. We have to humble ourselves enough and allow him to work the work in us. Prayers are designed to dig up all that dirt so that God can pour into us. Luke 5-36-39 says, "no one outs new wine into old wineskins, or else the old wine skins burst." So before God can really make us what he has already called us to be we have to let him deal with us on a deeper level so we can experience the true and living God.

As long as the enemy can keep us compromising who we are in Christ, we will never experience the dominion, the promise, and the fullness of God. We won't be able to walk in the full capacity that he has already ordained and given to us. The enemy does not want us to know who we are in Christ, and as we all know once we find that out we become a threat to the kingdom.

Leprosy means a powerful object of the debilitating influence of sin in a person's life. Leprosy is a graphic illustration of sin's destructive powers.

Debilitating means something that seriously affects someone or something's strength or the ability to carry on with regular activities. The Latin word means weak.

When God began to deal with me about the spirit of leprosy, it was very profound. It was enlightening because, in the biblical days, leprosy was a very severe disease that God gave Moses extensive instructions on how to deal with it, **Leviticus 13 & 14...** In my research leprosy was a horrible affliction. If anyone was suspected to have leprosy, they had to go before the priest to be checked. When the Bible speaks of leprosy, it appeared in two forms. Lepromatous was the first and foremost dangerous and Tuberculoid.

They both start with a discoloration of the skin, but Lepromatous was the type of leprosy that can spread in all directions of the body. It caused deformity of the hands and feet, and the tissues and the bones begin to deteriorate. Untreated cases may be sick for 20 years, and it was said that death could also occur. The Bible says that if they were diagnosed with leprosy they had to separate. They hung out with their kind until they were healed or either died.

Leviticus 13 45-46 says, "he shall remain unclean; he shall live alone. His dwelling shall be outside the camp." The person with leprosy was considered utterly unclean, physically and SPIRITUALLY. I asked God who are the type of people with leprosy?

He said people that have been molested, been mentally or sexually abused or grew up with no moral conduct or structure are emotionally torn. He said all of these barriers causes' emotional problems. Emotional means a spiritual effect; one day you up, the next day you down

Inner: Things you carry within

Psychological: Mental

Psychic: Is the heart the emotional needs that are often ignored?

If we can go back a few pages, I gave the history of the Israelites with leprosy from how they were treated to how they were separate from society. They had to cover their face, let their hair hang loose, and they hung out with each other. All day they walked around screaming I'm unclean! The king's said, "have not God bring these men because you think I can heal them." Another king came around and said, "but God can." That was the physical side we didn't know that it was a sign of what Jesus would do in the near future. Because what Moses couldn't do, Jesus will be able to carry out.

Now this is the Spiritual side...

Luke 17:11-19

Luke 17:11, "and it came to pass as he went to Jerusalem, that he passed through the midst of Samaria and Galilee." Luke 17:12, "and as he entered into a certain village, he met ten men that were lepers, which stood afar off." Luke 17:13 and they lifted up their voices and said, "Jesus, Master, have mercy on us." Luke 17:14, "and when he saw them, he said unto them, go shew yourselves unto the priests. And it came to pass, that, as they went, they were cleansed." Luke 17:15, "and one of them, when he saw that he was healed, turned back, and with a loud voice glorified God." Luke 17:16, "and fell down on his face at his feet, giving him thanks: and he was a Samaritan." Luke 17:17, and Jesus answering said, "were there not ten cleansed? But where are the nine?" Luke 17:18, "they've not returned to give glory to God, save this stranger." Luke 17:19, and he said unto him, "arise, go thy way: thy faith hath made thee whole."

Spiritual Attraction

Rejection= Rejecter Molestation=Molester Abuse=Abuser
Influence=Influencer Abandonment=Abandoner.

Let's take a look at our society; pedophiles, abusers, rejecters, murders, prostitutes, etc. It's a learned behavior... Why? Because they never got help. It's something that's rarely talked about in the church, but God loves them as well. God wants to help them as well; they aren't any different. Some in the mental hospital, some are in the pulpit, the choir stands, the jail, the music industry, let's face it, they're everywhere. I can't say it enough God came to save those that are lost not to judge, but to give life more abundantly. Somewhere in their life, they've been hurt. Maybe they saw mommy with different men; maybe they saw daddy packing and dealing dope, but somewhere in their life they were mishandled. It could be that they were taken advantage of sexually or they were abused mentally and/or emotionally. In some cases, they were just exposed to things that they should've never been exposed to (this is part of the moral conduct.)

IT AIN'T YOUR FAULT

So God says it's not your fault, for when I created you, I created you in an amazing way because it was after my own image. I had knowledge of you before you entered your mother's womb. I knew the way that you would take. I knew your ups, I knew your downs, I knew the tears you would shed, and I knew the heartaches you would experience. But it comes a time that we have to realize that we are sick spiritually; remember leprosy spreads throughout the whole body. When we are sick in our spirits, it spreads to our mind, our emotions, our hearts, and it also begins to affect our physical bodies. Depression makes us tired. We become unproductive, lazy, and unsuccessful. While repeating a vicious cycle, we also become self-destructive.So society has shaped us to believe we need medication or some other temporary fix. I struggle with that because God is the healer of all things.

I knew something was wrong with me because I was always angry, I wanted to die and attempted suicide numerous times... I got tired of going to church and coming out the same way I went in. I was still smoking blunt after blunt, ripping and running the streets, and hanging out at the bar with no regard for life. Oh, and of course I kept a man. I was doing hair making good money at 16 years old... I prayed I said, *"God you gotta help me!"* Remember the Israelites walked around screaming they were unclean... My self-destructive behavior was my way of screaming I am unclean. I said, "God you gotta lead me! I don't know where to go from here, but if you will just lead me!" Remember I told y'all I was raised in Detroit. I remember driving my blue Cavalier to Chandler Park; I sat there and I cried for about an hour…as I begin that prayer tears were streaming, I mean the thick tears. I started watching Christian networks and listening to gospel music. I use to leave the TV on all night. Well, one night I felt a presence; it felt like something was lifting me and it was resting on the top of my head. I looked towards the television and Marvin Winans was on TBN, testifying about how the Lord resurrected his dead brother Ron Winans. He said they were at St John Hospital praying that God will saSve his brother. He was pronounced dead, but God revived him! I never will forget it; he had on a red and black robe. The next Sunday, I did the same routine. I went to church; it was a family church, same service. After service was over, I was sitting in the parking lot rollin' up. Somehow, I got distracted so I didn't fire it up. I was rolling down 7 Mile Street and I looked up and saw a billboard with Marvin Winans on there. I started following the arrows and my God; I was in front of this big church. I made it just in time for the 3:00 service. As soon as I walked in, I started weeping uncontrollably. The choir began to sing God will keep you in perfect peace. I cried even more. I didn't know that Pastor Winans was going to be there. I didn't even know anything about him! Well, when they announced the pastor it was him. It was like when he stood up, his spirit looked like a father! It's hard to explain, but THERE WAS A CONNECTION! So I kept going, the third Sunday I went back to Perfecting Church and I made it to morning service. Again I am crying, this time I was screaming, and one of the ushers extended her hand, and it was leading to the altar. Well, something was pushing me. I mean this day was amazing! I had a long blonde ponytail, red lipstick, and lashes was thick for days with a green mini skirt on. I cried so hard I barely could see the altar. Pastor Winans had on this blue robe; it looked like he leaped off the pulpit and laid hands on me. I felt like I was in the cloud; I fell out real smooth and easy. He said, "pick her back up God wanna fill her with the holy spirit," and pastor tarried with me until I gave utterance and that was the beginning of a new life for me....

By this time I am working at Cutting Edge Hair Salon. I'm out here now, 17 years old, and got my own apartment. My first place was across the street from Denby High School. I was going thru it with my parents, I mean it was rough! Every day wasn't perfect; I fell short plenty of times, months, days, and years at a time. I've learned that it was a divine appointment that interrupted my life. A young lady by the name of Shonie started coming to get her hair done. She would always minister to me. One day she invited me to revival. I remember her talking about Mother Boyd. She would always say how powerful she is. I went to the service at Shalom Temple and Mother Boyd, Dr. Stacks, and Mother Dupree got a hold of me! They kept hitting me in the back and stomach. Then they had a garbage can and towels because I was puking everywhere. From that moment I was hooked. I went home, dyed my hair black, and bought all the long dresses I could find. That was the beginning of something great. I started sitting up under that good teaching. I learned how to fast and pray until you got a breakthrough and I learned how to really study the Bible. One day I went to prayer and I felt a strange feeling in my heart. It felt as if I couldn't go any further. It went on for a while so finally I asked Mother Stacks what it was. She said, "you at the fork in the road, which means God is ready to cross you over, but you have to deal with the issues in your heart." I really didn't understand that. Mother Stacks had an academy where she would train the young people in their gift. One day she asked for a young person to volunteer and of course, I raised my hand. She said, "okay we're going to see what you're working with!" That night God showed me this big silver bowl; some parts were clean and other parts had residue. God revealed to

16

me that was my spirit. The following weekend Mother Dupree came and she was conducting service. She said to me, "God wants to use you." I had no idea that I would be teaching my first message the following Sunday. Well, Sunday rolled around and it was time for me to give that word! My first message was titled, "Building a Temple for God." Mother Stacks said, "you got substance! You have something in that bell!" At this time, I was 19 years of age....

Well, after that message I somehow lost my way, I couldn't understand it! After careful consideration, I now know that I never dealt with those issues. You can be on fire for God and issues, sin, or iniquity in your heart can snatch you right down because the anointing needs to be able to rest in your heart. In the midst of all that, I got married! You know I married the wrong man right? I suffered dearly because I wasn't led by the spirit. I was led by emotions, lust, and issues. As they say, we attract who we are! I married a man that had issues such as the spirit of perversion. I had warnings, but I disobeyed God anyway. I didn't realize the danger of what I was doing. I added more hurt on top of issues that I still haven't dealt with. When we separated, the things he dealt with now became my issue. I got involved in a lot of perverseness, ripping and running the streets again, smoking blunt after blunt, and started meeting people of my kind! Remember earlier I mentioned how the people with leprosy hung out with their kind. The people I was hanging with had a background similar to mine so when we linked up, it was like we knew each other for a long time. At the age of 24, God blessed me with a salon, Optimistic Creations all while my marriage was going downhill. I mean it was a wreck! To cope, I started cheating and committing adultery, instead of letting God heal me. I guess I thought I found my own healing. When you are hurting full of issues, that's what you attract… you attract abusive men. Well in my case I attracted abusive men that had a drug problem and couldn't keep a job. If you're wondering why I didn't know how to choose a man, it's because as I previously mentioned we learn from what we see. I was always attracted to older men….Don't get me wrong I had a father in my later years after he got himself together. The thing is he wasn't an affectionate man. He was a good provider and he took care of me very well. So the affection I was missing at home, I looked for in older men. I looked for love, comfort, and the attention they were giving me. Of course, it was all the wrong attention, but I liked it at the moment. I saw my mother suffer those same things. The relationships I was in didn't last long because in my mind you're about to beat on me, not have a job, and think you're bout to come love on me! It wasn't happening. Before my husband and I completely separated we visited Shalom church. The service was so high! Sister Lumpy came over and prayed for me. She asked me, "why are you running? You're going to go through some things!" It was something pertaining to a shipwreck… She said, "you may not understand, but just hold on to God and continue to stay before him!" Well shortly after that I encountered another bad relationship; my first black eye! I tripped out, but it led me into prayer. The Lord began to deal with me in the book of Genesis, the story of Abraham. I'm just glad I had an ear to hear. About a month after that, I left I went to Birmingham Alabama, my birthplace. In my mind, this was an opportunity to get close with my mother since we've been away from each other for years. My mom signed her rights over to my father when I was very young. What I didn't think about was, that was the place where a lot of my hurt started and it was the root of some of the decisions I've made. Needless to say, that didn't work out. I left after two years of being there. I moved to Frankfort, Kentucky with my brother Brandon. I didn't understand why I went there, but now I see God was pulling me out of familiar places. He knew what it would take for me to seek him wholeheartedly. I had to be somewhere with no one to lean on, but him. As a result, this caused me to fast, pray, and seek him for direction yet; I haven't dealt with those issues. I began searching for a church home. I visited a few, but none felt like home to me. One day I spoke with a friend Terri and she said, "well you know Elder Curlin church is like three hours away." I was so desperate I didn't care! Every other Sunday I drove down to his church in Hopkinsville, Kentucky and it was so amazing! I went up for prayer during the altar call, and Elder Curlin spoke something to me that nobody knew, but God. He didn't know I was diagnosed with bipolar disorder. He had no idea that I had been in a mental hospital. He said, " God is going to heal your mind! He's gone heal you down to the depths of your soul! At that moment, I knew that's where I needed to be. They had prayer every day, and I was used to that…. and most of all this man saw something that no one could really see in the spirit. I mean a few people did, but I didn't sit long enough to get the full deliverance, so when I look back, I was running from the pain it hurt too much to deal with it. So I moved again because I was determined to know who I was in God and my purpose. It wasn't easy; I had a lot of strange days so strange that I took matters into my own hands because I still haven't dealt with those issues. I felt like I didn't have anyone. I was at a very low place. I was used to a certain lifestyle and you know I felt like I had to keep my fronts up. I can't let anybody see me sweating. In my mind, I gotta' get some money and make it happen! It took me awhile to adapt because I grew up in a big city and every day it's a hustle, hook, or crook. I had that mentality when I got to Hoptown. I got a job in Clarksville. Elder saw God blessing me with a job and needless to say I had plenty to choose from. Everything I experienced was designed for me to trust God. Sometimes we get frustrated and go off track and that's a dangerous place to be! You have now stepped outside of the will of God. Just when I thought I escaped my issues, I got involved in another bad relationship. This one almost took me up out of here. That's why it's so important that we allow God to heal us and clean us up. Now carnally we had a lot in common. We both grew up fast and liked old school music such as Johnny Taylor, and The Isley Brothers. Both of us did a huge amount of drugs and were hustlers. We had mommy issues, so it was like we fed off each other, but it was unhealthy. The relationship was designed to take my identity. It took me from who I was trying to become in God. That spirit of perversion that I thought was gone had now resurfaced. I was depressed, sad, didn't wanna take care of myself, just bad. He was abusive and we were constantly fighting. IT was a degrading relationship, but to be honest, it seems as if I liked it because it looked normal. That's what I saw with my mom. I allowed all of that to consume my true identity. Some mornings I would press my way to prayer and Mother Turner would always speak something to my spirit. I was ashamed, and I felt that I had failed God, myself, as well as others because of the assignment that God had given me. A simple assignment it was. Prayer! I remember asking God, "what's wrong with me?" I was in tears I said, "It can't be like this! Something has to be done. I keep falling when I don't wanna fall. I'm being pushed further than I wanna go. GOD HELP ME!" He delivered me out of that relationship, but because of the strong soul ties I ended up right back. I thought I could have him and God and make it work. Well, it got worse and worse; I was in a horrible pit. I couldn't pull myself

21

out, but because I disobeyed God again so I had to ride it out. God knew the way that I would take. He knew I was going to mess up. Fear had gripped me; I was scared of being alone. I didn't have any family; I couldn't tell anybody what I was going through. I was in the danger zone. I started pressing to church, pressing in prayer at my home, and I watched the hand of God come in and deliver me. I'm so thankful; that relationship made me seek God on so many different levels. It forced me to deal with those issues, and it brought me to a place of confidence and knowing who I am in God. When you know who you are in God, nothing can stop you! There is a confidence that He gives you. You won't find yourself being caught up because you'll know that's not what God says about you. You won't let another man or any situation define who you are or take from you. You won't be jealous of any. You won't try to be like the next person because you are who you are and uniquely made. I was abused sexually so much when I was younger; I didn't know my value. I didn't know how to appreciate me so when a man approached me in my mind all he wanted is sex. The things I experienced sexually at a young age caused me to be loose in my moral conduct. So society (The Devil) taught me how to make money doing it. At the age of 14, I was sneaking around doing private parties. At just 14 years old, I had my first encounter making money for sexual exchange and it became a habit. In that life, there aren't no strings attached; it's a fantasy world. All of this came about because I had no one to protect me. Mommy was gone, daddy was gone, and my sister and I moved from house to house. I remember my daddy saying he was going to see a lawyer and he never came back. I sat on the floor many days asking my auntie,

22

"where is my daddy?" It's almost like I didn't have any family. I didn't know what it was like; this is where abandonment issues set in, fear of being alone, not feeling wanted. Previously we talked about pre- conventional moral conduct.. These are the years that are so important and valuable because it shapes who we are and what we will become. This is where I will say that both parents are to be present because that's the way God intended it to be. God never intended for a woman too be single raising their children alone. He gave us structure through his word. God designed the woman (wife) to be mentors to teach younger women to be sober and love their children. God designed the man (husband) to be the head of the household, the overseer, the protector, and the provider. Abandonment leads to unhealthy relationships; it leads to self-destructive behavior, drugs, and suicide. Some of these things become a comfort zone; it's a form of escaping reality. Rejection can cause you to do things out of the ordinary cause you try to settle for things or someone that's just not meant to be a part of your life, and you do things to keep the connection out of fear of being alone or just wanting to be loved. I found myself abandoning myself from the church often because I didn't want anyone to see my pain, my flaws. I wanted people to think I had it together, but really I was a wreck. I dressed accordingly so I felt if I looked a certain way or lived a certain way no one will detect that I am so broken on the inside. For a long time, I ran from the pain. I covered it by doing heavy drugs and having sex. I never wanted to be alone; I felt like I had to have a companion. I had to be high, making myself regurgitate after I eat and that was self-destructive behavior. He delivered my soul from the battles that were against me and they were many. He lifted me from the pit of destruction out of the miry clay, and set my feet upon a rock, and established my goings.

Ellington Village

Ellington Village was a nightmare. My mother was dating this guy who's name was Mr. Jones. He was a painter and also abusive. Mr. Jones loved to fight my mother. Things were so intense my mom would come into our room and tell us she loved us in case she didn't make it through the night. I would just lay there with tears in my eyes thinking, "what are we going to do? This man is crazy!" We didn't have heat most of the time, no electricity, no water, no food, and when we did have food the rats were in it. Then his son, Mr. Smokey moved in. He had his way with me; I was so young, I hadn't even started my menstrual. He did horrible things to me like urinating on me and inside me. I was disgusted; my mother always left us there with him. I told my mother and she didn't do anything. Well, she took me to the doctor. I guess I contracted something because they gave her cream and a tube. She didn't really explain what it was for; I would lay across the bed and she would insert it inside of me. The sexual abuse from Mr. Smokey didn't stop. I didn't get to see anyone. She kept us away from family and forced us not to tell what went on. Our living situation was so jacked up. I was embarrassed when my friends would walk home with me. They would ask where do you stay? I would always try to pick the nicest house on the block and hope they wouldn't see me go into my real house. My dad sent for us in the summertime. When summer was over, I would dread going back to that house. I couldn't tell anyone why because she threatened us. I would go in the bathroom and pray, "God, please take this situation from us. Make these men go away God please, please God." The following Sunday we went to church. I remember it like it was yesterday. I was to young to understand what the preacher was saying, but the choir was singing an old hymn, "I love the Lord." He heard my cry; I wept the rest of the service. Later that week Mr. Jones beat my mom again. This time was the worst I've ever seen. Her eyes were black and her teeth were gone. For days after that, I watched her mope around the house all the time listening to Denise Williams, "love oh love stop making a fool of me." A few days later Mr. Jones and Mr. Smokey was gone. Then we went to stay with my Aunt Linda over in Ensley. We didn't see mommy for a while. When she came back, we moved to Pratt City. We stayed behind my grandfather's house. For that to have been her father, there wasn't much communication. Not too long after, my mommy got in another relationship. Things seemed ok for the moment. His name was Mr. Starks; beer drinking, cigarette smoking, Mr. Starks. I wanted to fight him. He's laid up in our house not buying groceries and my mom barely worked. I was really upset because it was Christmas time. My sister and I woke up to nothing. …..so we thought. There was a knock on the door. It was my grandma dropping off gifts that my father had sent us. I was so happy! At this point, I didn't know how to feel about my mom. We left that house and moved down the street from my now deceased grandma Jackie. She died of cancer. Mr. Starks had full control now. I've reached a point where I was very vocal and angry. I stood up to Mr. Starks because he thought he was going to hit on me. He's not my daddy! My vocal self would tell him that. One day he was sitting on the couch drinking beer while my mother was gone to work. My sister and I were cleaning up. As I was cleaning

26

up, I dropped the table salt by mistake. He says, "drop it again!" Now I'm nervous because he was picking on me. In my nervousness, I dropped the salt again, He jumped up, took his belt off, and whipped me, but me being me, I still was running off at the mouth. I didn't do anything so I'm going to run my mouth to give you a reason to whip me. Living there was a trip; they were trifling. Their bedroom smelled like a nursing home and no one was even sick or bedridden. They were too lazy to go to the bathroom so they had a piss pot in the middle of the floor and my sister and I had to empty it. One day Grandma Jackie walked down there and she never came down there. She went in my mother's room and she asked her what was wrong with her. Grandma smelled that urine and saw the bucket. Oh my God, Grandma Jackie went off! We never had to empty that bucket again. It's a constant thing with Mr. Starks and I. Every time she left us he picked on me. I was going to Mawcaw Elementary School; I was in the 4th grade. One Wednesday morning I was getting ready for school; my mother came in the bathroom and she said, "I am going send you to your father for a while." I was so happy! I was like "OK!" She says, "your flight leaves Sunday." I was like "COOL." I believe he told her to get rid of me because when she took me to the airport, she was crying. As I've gotten older, I believe it was because she made a horrible decision and that was choosing her man over me........

Depression Suicide

So I arrive in Detroit, and there is my hero, my father. ...What I
didn't know before I left is my mother had signed her rights over to
my father. When I was told, I didn't believe it until my aunt showed
me the papers. I was in the 5th grade; I attended Stellwagen
Elementary School. Elementary was cool; I was in a lot of activities,
I ran track, was involved in the writers club, and was in a singing
group (yes I can sing.) So at that moment, it seemed as if the
gloomy days were over! I had an opportunity to participate in things
I never had down south. My cousin Aretha always had something
going on because she ran a daycare business. After I graduated from
elementary, I attended Hamilton Middle School. I met some good
friends. Middle school was different because that's when my self-
destructive behavior set in. I started smoking weed, skipping school,
and attempting suicide...taking pills, cutting my arms, but GOD! I
wanted to feel loved and I wasn't getting it. I figured if I just die I
wouldn't have to endure any pain. Although, I had family around I
still felt out of place. Deep down inside I was longing for my
mother. I saw my friends with their mom; I wanted my mom too. I
had to just settle for what life had dealt to me. By the time I
graduated Hamilton it was a good feeling. I had a chance to sing at
our graduation. I sang a song by my favorite girl Whitney Houston,
The Greatest Love Of All. At that moment, my father was dating
someone and I can admit I felt some type of way. I felt like I was
losing him. I guess he deserves to be happy. Shortly after I
graduated from Hamilton, we moved to the west side and we were
like any other family arguing, fighting etc. My stepmom had kids

from a previous relationship. No relationship is perfect; we had our moments, but she always encouraged me. She gave me freedom to express myself and she understood me. I was very rebellious when I got to high school. I truly didn't care what was going on. My mind was on skipping school, getting high, and going to cosmetology class. I don't know how I graduated. I attended Crockett High School. I found a way to escape reality and that was getting high, drinking, out of control doing private parties for pay, and working at McDonald's. I always kept some type of hustle going. Eleventh grade was very trying for me; I was dealing with suicide a lot. I got to the point where I just didn't care. One day I almost succeeded.... My stepmom was in the hospital, my sister and I had a fight, and my boyfriend at the time broke my heart. I got as high as I could, took as many pills as I could, and I passed out. All I remember is waking up in the hospital tied to the bed. In between passing out and waking up, I was in a dark tunnel. I could hear the doctors talking over me, but I wasn't responding. I could here the ministers praying over me, but I still wasn't responding. When I snapped back, they were escorting me to the mental hospital. They had me tied up like I was a criminal. Well, I guess I was a criminal to myself. God wasn't willing to let me go out like that. Being in that hospital was a sad occasion for me. God sent Darlene to come pray. When she prayed for me she said, "you're coming home. You going to be alright." My roommate at the hospital became my buddy. We supported each other. Her father was raping her on a regular. We cried and prayed together many nights there. One day they sent me to talk to a counselor to prescribe me with meds. I went in there and he said, "I am supposed to give you some pills to help with your problems, but I am not going to do this to you. I'm going to let you go home." It was two days before Christmas. When I got home, I called my best friend Kym. She caught the bus to where I was. We went to the beauty supply and she did my hair for me. I love her to death for that! She didn't judge me or call me crazy like everyone else. At that moment, I knew our friendship was solid. On top of the fact that the snow was unreal lol and that was a lot of walking, but she was there for me.

I thank God every day for where I am today. Situations and different challenges will come our way, but we cannot let them consume us. It's a sad thing when leaders in the church are killing themselves. People with great missions are dying!

It took a lot for me to release this book, but in the midst of it, I did a lot of crying. There were days that I just didn't want to channel the pain. I thank God for the pain. *It's because of that I now know that I am who God says I AM…*

Special thanks to God my friend
because he gave me the courage!

Lets Us Pray Together

I am what God says; I am prayer.

I am a royal priest hood a chosen generation.

A holy nation; a peculiar people (individual).

I am a partaker of his promise in Christ by the gospel. I am a minister according to the gift of the grace of God given unto me the effectual working of his power.

I am a living epistle; I am an example of Christ not by letter or stone, but by the spirit.

I am enriched by him in all utterance and in all knowledge. I am redeemed; I am the head and not the tail. I am above and not beneath.

I am an overcomer by the blood of the lamb.

I am whole; I am complete in him. I am somebody; when he created me it was a wonderful thing.

"I Am What God Says I Am"

My current Situation

So now I am back home in Detroit. It's been a year since I have been back from Nashville...and that process was interesting because I opened a salon in Nashville...The landlord didn't want to renew the lease... now I have to figure out..what am I going to do because I stayed 40 minutes away from the salon..So I needed direction. I got into prayer and was led to move back to Michigan..I never thought I would come back..but God has been very true to his word....and has been my sole provider since I been back.

So now the struggle is real because now that I know who I am in God..now that I know my purpose..it's a battle... I know the old me, the old Rashelle, I'm very familiar with her...But this new Rashelle the one that God has called me to be... I really don't know her....so the battle is now allowing him to work his perfect will in me.........Because of the things I went through, I am more conscious who I deal with. I am more prayerful and not so quick to let a man rule and dominate my true identity in Christ...I can boldly say that I am learning how to fall in love with Jesus.. I am learning how to love me; I am learning how to let God love me..Every day I am pressing toward the mark.. Everyday ain't great..But I am learning.....

I am learning that when you ask God to change you..when you ask God to perfect everything that concerns you... you best believe there's a major shift coming.. From your job all the way around the board... God says, "when we come to the knowledge of him..our life, our new life is hidden in him....How do we find that life.... A simple prayer.. Lord let thy will be done...Meaning whatever your will is for me, Lord let it be.... Lord, here I am; I'm willing to put my desires aside to carry out your perfect plan for my life....

I don't know all that God has in store for me..but I feel something great..Keep me in prayer and follow me as I learn how to walk in the fullness that God has called me to operate in...

I love you all because God said so…....

www.ingramcontent.com/pod-product-compliance
Lightning Source LLC
Chambersburg PA
CBHW060203070426
42447CB00033B/2374